HOT SEAT CONVERSATIONS

GET TIPS, GET NOTICED, GET GOING

BY

CARRIE HARTUNIAN SMITH

Acknowledgments

I wanted to acknowledge and thank the following, for being instrumental to my success and the success of this book:

God, for allowing me to wake up every morning and ask, "How can I honor You today?"

My Family, specifically my son and my parents, for supporting me in ways only family can during these transition years.

Mike Koenigs, Ed Rush and Pam Hendrickson for creating the amazing programs that have allowed me to grow personally and professionally.

Traffic Geyser/Instant Customer Sales and Support Staff who always respond to my emails and phone calls, faithfully, no matter what my question.

The TG/IC Amazing Community and Masterminds, without your support along the way, (sometimes daily!) carrying on would have been much more difficult.

And to all the interviewees who made the time in their busy schedules to help create this book... Thank you!

Table of Contents

Introduction

If you've ever been around a Live Event with Mike Koenigs and company , (produced by Jessie Schwartzburg) you know 'it's the place to be!'. These events are 2-3 days packed full of content that will launch your business further than you ever imagined. You'll find high energy, upbeat music, fun videos, and fabulous people to meet and reconnect with! This is a community like no other!

You ask how do I know? Well, I can tell you first hand, after 'joining' this community my lack luster consulting business went from barely having a monthly revenue stream to that of one close to 6-figures, did I mention, in less than 3 months?

There is no magic, or get rich quick schema at these events ... just solid marketing principals, taught in a way that will change in your life, both personally and professionally, assuming you implement.

One of the segments that makes these events life changing are called Hot Seats.

With the competition for Hot Seat positions being fierce it's important to really understand the benefits of participating in the Hot Seat so you can properly apply for one of those coveted positions.

If you are anxiously waiting for your time on stage, this book is for you. If you need a little more encouragement or confidence to take that step, this book is also for you. This book is for anyone who wants to be prepared for a Hot Seat so that they can extract as much benefit from the experience as possible.

I've sat down and interviewed some of my favorite Hot Seat participants – the ones with the greatest stories, greatest people and with the greatest lessons to teach us. The trailblazers, if you will. I interviewed these people on how the Hot Seat as changed their lives – and asked them to provide insight on how you can make the most of your Hot Seat experience.

Lastly, before we get started, head over to my website and grab a free download containing some of the tips that are shared in each chapter:

READ THIS BEFORE APPLYING FOR YOUR HOT SEAT by clicking on this link:

www.YourBookBonus.com

You will also be subscribed to my newsletter - which is fun, informative and all about making sure you have a great Live Event experience.

If you've been on a Hot Seat and would like to be featured in 'Hot Seat Conversations' Vol 2, be sure to visit www.YourBookBonus.com

Chapter 1
Hot Seat?! What's That!

Webster's Dictionary: noun

> a position of uneasiness, embarrassment, or anxiety

Urban Dictionary:

> to put someone on the spot.

Mike's Possible Definition:

> A deep dive into your business

***

You might be asking yourself, **if** I was interested ... how would I find myself up on stage with these marketing genius?

It all starts with filling out a simple form and turning it into the back of the room before a designated time. Info like Name, cell #, your website, and where you are from.

Then it gets a little deeper.

- Tell a little about yourself and your business idea
- Are you an expert/authority, if so, in what?
- What are your credentials or experience in this area?
- Are you an author or product creator? If so please provide the title of your book or product.
- What is your immediate business goal?
- What 3 areas do you most need help?
- And the fun one ... write something unique or fun about yourself!

Once the form is filled out and turned in, you wait to see if you are selected. Anytime I've ventured back to see how many forms are in the basket, it's safe to say the basket is overflowing! With event attendance around 300 people, my guess is over 100 forms are submitted during an event. Now, there are only 2-3 Hot Seat Applications selected per day. So if my math is correct, well I'm not great at math, but let's just say earning your way on stage can be difficult. The more interesting you/your story is, the better chance you have to make it up on stage!

Don't let this discourage you from moving forward though, I just want to point out this opportunity is a 'Hot' commodity! And be sure you are prepared in every way possible for what could quite possibly be the single most thing that transforms your life!

Now, for the questions that are not on the application that ALWAYS are asked on stage:

- Who is your Avatar (and no, not the Blue people from the Block Buster Hit from 2009)

- Tell your story. Make it compelling, tell us how you changed someone's life

You might be asked:

- What do you do?

- Who do you do it for?

- And What makes you different!?

This is where it will be really beneficial for you to have several benefit driven statements ready to share about your business or product, not just listing the features.

This might sound real simple to some, but to others, well, you might be thinking ...YIKES! No matter if this is simple or not, the question is are your prepared to make the most out of this amazing time you will have on stage?

Before you take the next steps to 'deep dive into your business', take a look at what some of the Hot Seat Alumni have to share with you.

Get ready to build your brand and business bigger than ever!

TO LEARN MORE ABOUT EACH OF OUR SUCCESSFUL HOT SEAT EXPERTS

VISIT WWW.YOURBOOKBONUS.COM

SEE WHAT SPECIAL BONUS' ARE WAITING FOR YOU!

WWW.YOURBOOKBONUS.COM

www.facebook.com/CarrieHartunianSmith

Chapter 2
It's Never Too Late

Let me introduce you to Joni Wilson. Joni is a three-time best-selling author and, a self-proclaimed 'voice nut,' she is a recognized voice expert, trainer and coach.

Joni's passion for the voice is palpable as she explained to the audience during her Hot Seat how a person's voice could make or break a career, impact your personal and professional life, and ultimately effect your future and success. Regardless of your career path, your voice is an instrumental piece of your presentation.

Joni and I have never met, I was simply enthralled with her Hot Seat recording and was able to track her down to her Voice Studio on 54th Street in San Diego, California. I know that once you hear her story that her personality and fun-loving spirit will move you.

Below is Joni's interview on how she prepared for, not one, but two Hot Seats in the same weekend.

Hot Seat

Carrie: How many Mike/Pam events have you attended?

Joni: My first one was February 2014 in San Diego and that is where I was on the hot seat; that is the one that I was selected for. It was my first event. I was kind of a newbie to the group. It is an amazing group. I went, just to see what it was all about.

Carrie: Why and what prompted you to apply to a hot seat; what did you hope to get from the experience?

Joni: You have to understand that even though I've been in show business my entire life, when it comes to things like these – I'm not one of those people who thinks of applying for the Hot Seat. But, I was sitting next to a lady who filling out the questionnaire and she was explaining to me what an opportunity the Hot Seat was and sort of pressured me to also apply. It made sense, so I went, Oh, Okay and wrote it out and turned it in.

What did I hope to get out of it.... I hoped to not get called, that was my main goal! When I applied, I was pretty much telling myself that it was okay because they weren't going to call me and so I didn't really have to worry about it.

But, when I applied my problem (or what I hoped to get out of it) was that as a voice teacher I get paid to teach by the hour – how in the world do you break out of a cycle where you are always working for your next paycheck and are limited by the number of hours available?

Carrie: Mike is always talking about keeping things interesting and engaging; do you recall what the fun factor was; or why you were selected to be on the hot seat?

Joni: Well, my first job as a singer, was as an opening act to Elvis and that really gets people's attention – so I don't think that hurt. I am also not the youngest person at the event, I come from a whole different generation and there are not a lot of us that are out there trying to reinvent ourselves. So my fun factor was the Elvis thing and my age.

Carrie: What suggestions might you have for someone who wants to stand out from other applications they receive?

Joni: Bare your soul. Some people go up there to promote their business and you can tell when they get up there, that is all they talk about and then other people go up there to really genuinely get information. The thing about a hot seat is, when you have got experts like Ed, Pam, Mike, and Paul and they are all sitting up there wanting to help you; you have got to give them a problem, because that is what they are there for; they are there to solve your problem.

So my suggestion would be that you put down what the problem is, mine as I said was working by the hour and it was kind of embarrassing for me to say; I am really successful, I have got three best-selling books, and people come from all over the world to work with me, but two years ago I filed for bankruptcy. That kind of made me interesting I think. They went, whoa, there is a really good problem to solve. So give them something to work with; do not tell them how wonderful you are because that is not why you are on the hot seat; you are on the hot seat, so they can help you solve your problem; and hopefully it will help someone else, who has the same problem.

Carrie: In general, what do you think the biggest challenge is for people once on stage?

Joni: The biggest challenge is not talking about yourself; the people that get up there and their main function is to let people know how wonderful they are and what their business is, with the hope that maybe they will get clients out of being in the hot seat; that is not what it is there for. The hot seat is there, as I said, to share your story in the hopes that it might actually help someone else. Once you get on there, the biggest challenge is really telling your story and not trying to embellish it, or cover it over but just really, really saying what it is that you need help with; because you are sitting there, with amazing experts whose business is helping people and they are the best at it.

Carrie: Do you have suggestions on how to overcome that challenge?

Joni: Yeah, you have to kind of depersonalize; you cannot think of "wow they will think I am a big failure," or you cannot go up there worried about what people are going to think of you. You go up there to share an experience.

Carrie: What and how do you think is the best way to prep for a hot seat?

Joni: Well mine was interesting, because I was up there on a Saturday, baring my soul, and Pam told me that she wanted me to go home, write a pitch and get back up there on Sunday and pitch the business to them in front of everyone. She got two people to volunteer to work with me to get it done – but, the overachiever that I am – I sat down and I wrote out my whole speech and then began to try and memorize it.

I kept thinking, I am okay. They aren't going to call me up until the end of the day, so I have time. I came back from lunch and Mike said, "Is Joni out in the audience?" and I raised my hand. He said, "You're next!", and I went uhhh, I do not have it memorized, what am I going to do; and I thought, just do not think; do not think, do not think, you know everything there is to know about the voice, you know who you are, you just go up there, and you be yourself; which is exactly what I did. I went up there and I totally forgot everything that I had written.

Thankfully they take you by the hand and they will lead you right where you need to go. It was a beautiful experience. I mean I said things that I did not even write in my speech, I do not even know what said.

When I came back down the people said, you did really well! I was like oh thank you, I do not know what I did but oh well! It was fun.

Okay so I would say, that how do you prepare; you do not, you just trust those beautiful people, that are up there on the stage with you, to make you look good, because they will, they will pull it out of you, so do not worry; do not prepare.

Carrie: Can you share one of the most impactful moments you had while on stage?

Joni: The most impactful moment that I had is just exactly the one that I just said, when I got up there and I had to leave my beautiful written script on my seat and just go by the seam of my pants, and trust; and they were wonderful, that was the scariest moment; I actually thought about, at noon on Sunday, I was actually thinking about getting in my car because I live in San Diego and the event was in San Diego, and I thought if I go home and they call my name and I am not there, they will just think maybe I got sick, or maybe had an emergency or something and I will not have to go through this; but I went oh no, no, no, no Wilson, you have got to do this; you have got to do it, so I stayed and I did it.

Carrie: How did you specifically benefit from you hot seat?

Joni: It just totally turned my life around. You never know at that point, when you sign up, you have no idea; you cannot go up there with expectations of, oh I am going to promote my book, I am going to promote myself, I am going to promote my business; that is not it, you go up with your soul to bare, in the hopes that your problem, whatever it is will benefit someone else and I will tell you the truth, it really, really will, but most of all, it will benefit you.

Carrie: If you could turn back the clock, what would be the one or two things, you would like to do over?

Joni: I would never go home, and write myself a script. I wasted so much time; I even had a hard time on Sunday morning concentrating on what was going on, because I was thinking, I have to go memorize my script, I have to go memorize my script.

Don't go out there with any preconceived notions. Just clear your mind and put your trust, basically where you put your trust; whether it is in God, whether it is in the universe, or whatever it is; you just turn that over to someone else or something else or something more powerful than you, or even better still; you turn it over to those amazing people sitting on that stage with you and you trust that they are going to make you look good and they will, they will.

Carrie: If you were to provide one or two tips to someone, who is either thinking about or planning to fill out a hot seat hot seat form, to help them get the most out of the experience; what piece of advice would you provide in an effort to help them prepare and get the best out of the hot seat?

Joni: Again, I would say that the best advice that I could give, is trust the people that are on stage with you; do not over think it. Just put yourself in their hands and just trust; they are the experts and they will bring out of you what they need to bring out of you.

Carrie: Finally tell us; how are things going with you now and how did the hot seat help you with your business?

Joni: It just turned my life around, as I said; since then I have created a new generation; I did not just create a business, I created a prime time generation and I took my generation, which is the greatest generation of the thirties and forties and I combined it with the first world baby boomers. It is everybody that walks through that portal into the second half of their life and turns around, looks around and says oh my gosh, what do I do now?

There is so much to do, especially in this world now, because all the world is your stage; and you have got video and pod casting and writing your book and all these amazing things that you can do to get your information out that was not there when I first started and it is all there for us now; and we just have to reach out, and have the courage to grab it.

So I would say, if you are considering doing the hot seat, or considering not doing it: do it. Do it because it will change your life. It is the most amazing experience, you will love it.

It may be 'hot' up on stage, and it may be a little bit hot on your rare end, sitting up there with them looking at you, going why did you do this, why did you do that; but it sure makes you think and it sure makes you really consider what it is that you are doing. Then from that, you just go for it; it gets your momentum and your juices; it gets everything in you, thinking and going forward, and you go for it, you just go for it, do not be afraid.

Joni: Thank you for asking me to share and I hope my experience will help another person make up their mind to get right up there, and be on that hot seat.

To learn more about Joni Wilson visit
www.virtualvoicecoach.com

TO LEARN MORE ABOUT EACH OF OUR SUCCESSFUL HOT SEAT EXPERTS

VISIT
WWW.YOURBOOKBONUS.COM

SEE WHAT SPECIAL BONUS' ARE WAITING FOR YOU!

WWW.YOURBOOKBONUS.COM
www.facebook.com/CarrieHartunianSmith

Chapter 3
Messy in the Middle

Joe has been around the Mike Koenigs community for a little while having been to a few events. In February 2014 was his first Hot Seat, during Instant Customer.

When Joe and I spent some time talking through the concept of Hot Seats, he passed along a comment that had been shared with him ... 'everything is always messy in the middle.'

He went on to say, "Think of a surgery, you walk in the room prior to surgery and after it's over, everything is clean and neat. But when you walk in during the surgery ... its messy, bloody, gory. It's a disaster!"

For Joe, the beginning and end are his comfort zone. When he is in the middle, its way outside his comfort zone! He related his time on the Hot Seat being smack dab in the middle of surgery!

Let's take a look at how Joe explains his experience and view of what comes out of Hot Seats during these live events.

The Hot Seat

Carrie: Having been around the events somewhat regularly, I would imagine you had a pretty good understanding how they work and what can come from Hot seats, what did that look like for you?

Joe: You know I have seen a wide range of people an experiences; there are some people, they just look like they are just absolutely ready to go; and then there is the people that are deer in the headlights; and I knew I was not ready to go, but I did not want to be the deer either.

Carrie: Why did you decide to do a hot seat; what did you hope to get out of it?

Joe: Oh, I think a couple things; you know, the sound of one hand clapping. You get in your own head about something and how do you get any objective feedback much less good feedback? So, as an entrepreneur sometimes you try to figure something out in your head, doing everything inside, and never letting the world see it until you think it is ready. That is just not healthy on any level, and I am guilty of that.

You have these smart people [Mike, Pam, Ed, Paul] that are willing to help, want to help, and you need help; and a room full of people that are wishing the best for you.

Carrie: Right, so it's the idea of taking advantage of a fabulous opportunity; cease the moment kind of thing!

Joe: And then every bit of you is like, nooo...it is just the most uncomfortable thing that you can volunteer to do. So I kept thinking about what a great opportunity it was and I tried to ignore my feelings, and just did it.

Carrie: Do not think about anything, clear your mind and go...

Joe : Right; it is something that I have had to learn. Before, if I did something it was for a specific purpose – most because I wanted to win. I am a competitive person, I grew up as an athlete; so whatever I was doing was with the purpose to win and now it is more like it is the purpose to do as absolutely best as you can and take what comes.

Carrie: Whenever I go to these events there could be anywhere from three hundred plus people and anytime. I always go to the back to check out the basket where people submit their Hot Seat application. There are usually more than a hundred submitted; and I have always wondered what are people doing to be the ones picked. Do you have any suggestions for someone who really wants to get up on stage?

Joe : I think that the thing that attracts me most to this community and I think the thing that is the main ingredient in your success is being authentic. If you are authentic, I think you will fit in really well there. That does not mean you have to be like everyone else, but you have to be you.

Carrie: I like that... I think sometimes people can, not be themselves, just to get to a certain place, and it shows through.

Joe: Yeah, and I think that it does show through. There are a lot of things I like about Mike; I think he can smell BS from a pretty fair distance away. When they read an application; they know who is authentic and who isn't.

Carrie: What do you think the biggest challenge is for people once they actually get up on stage?

Joe: Talking; and when I mean talking I mean; how do you have a discussion with three people in front of other hundreds of other people. How do you talk to them and just talk to them authentically. Again, being authentic.

Carrie: So almost like, forget that the audience is there and just be you.

Joe: Yeah, if they do not know you and they are trying to build a personal solution for you; then if you show them an inaccurate image of yourself; the solution would not be right for you.

Carrie: Yeah, good point. How did you prepare yourself to be on the hot seat?

Joe : It was one of those times when an opportunity presented itself and you have to decide what choice you are going to make: Are you going to make a choice based on your fears and insecurities? If so, then you got to live with that and that is a very uncomfortable feeling. So I just took the application and despite not knowing what I was going to write - I just wrote what came out of my heart. That afternoon, I get a call from Jessie who tells me I'm going to be a panelist.

So you have this opportunity….

Carrie: Do it.

Joe: You have to just do it! I do not want to be a fear based person, so I submitted the application and I just trusted that what is going to happen is going to happen.

Carrie: So share with me one of the most impactful moments that you had while you were on stage.

Joe: I love watching the way these guys; the way their gears work. Mike; he looks at things one way; and that is a great perspective, but Pam has a much different perspective and Paul has a different perspective. It is like if I am sitting with my buddies and I am having a beer and we are all talking freely; and when you feel that at ease – the energy and the ideas begin to feed off one another.

Carrie: That's great insight.

Joe: So; I kind of thought; Mike is kind of edgy too; which is good, because even though I look a little reserved I can be very edgy and he kind of smelled that on me. You could throw things at me and it does not bother me at all; I am used to it. Pam; she is just really professional, and she has got a certain warmth to her and Paul, I love his humor, but in this humor there is always some good ideas.

Carrie: Yeah he does; he will come out with some really creative concepts or ideas.

Joe: Yeah, so if you can just like relax and just pretend you are having a beer with your friends and let it go and let the whole process be, and be uncomfortable with asking questions like 'what do you mean by that?' Instead of just going back to the deer in the headlights.

The hot seat was a catalyst. You can sit in the audience and be anonymous forever, but once you take action; you will have to change – You've already made the first step.

Carrie: If you were to provide one or two tips to someone who was either thinking about or definitely planning to fill out that hot seat form; what advice would you give them to really help get the most out of their experience?

Joe: Be completely honest, and do not over think it.

Carrie: Wow I like that; do not over think it, because we can complicate it right?

Joe: Yeah and you can; once you start trying to be something else; I think so many times we can out smart ourselves, just do it; just trust.

Carrie: So, I really appreciate you giving me your experience and feedback from the hot seat, but probably one of the most exciting questions, that I have been waiting to ask is; tell me, tell the readers; how are things going for you now, and how did the hot seat transform your life or your business?

Joe: Well I was telling the truth when I said I didn't know what I would write when I sat down to complete my application. I was having a problem with two businesses and I did not know which one I wanted to bring up. So I chose one and went up there without a plan – but with an idea of what I would do if I ever had it all to do over again. So, after the presentation there was a break and someone came up to me and said, I would like to hire you right now.

Carrie: Nice!

Joe: I am ready to go, he says. Can you do this right now in California?

Carrie: Can you share what business that is, so in case anyone reading this, needs someone of your expertise, they can seek you out?

Joe: Well yes, I can, it is real estate.

Carrie: Okay

Joe: But the funnier part is, that the other business was marketing.

Carrie: Okay

Joe: And the truth is; is that they are really the same business, I just could not fit it all in my head at the same time, and only know after we came from that last conference did I get the 'aha!' moment; where I know how to work them together the way they should, and have the message come out the way it should.

Carrie: That is awesome; all that from a 'little' twenty minute conversation on a hot seat.

Joe : Isn't that amazing?

Carrie: Isn't that amazing; so Joe if someone wanted to reach out to you, to have you help them along their journey, how would someone do that?

Joe: my personal email; joe@joequartana.com.

Carrie: Joe I really appreciate your time, and again, you gave definitely a different perspective than I have heard from some of the people that I have talked to about hot seats, and I think that just goes to show you that we are all individuals struggling with different things, succeeding with different things. To hear your perspective, I am sure will touch somebody in the audience and help them to take action the way they need to as you said. So I appreciate you being vulnerable and really opening up for this interview. I look forward to following back up with you in the future to see how your life is continuing to change and transform.

Joe: Thank you Carrie.

Carrie: I appreciate your words of wisdom.

To learn more about Joe Quartana, send an email to
Joe@Joequartana.com

TO LEARN MORE ABOUT EACH OF OUR SUCCESSFUL HOT SEAT EXPERTS

VISIT
WWW.YOURBOOKBONUS.COM

SEE WHAT SPECIAL BONUS' ARE WAITING FOR YOU!

WWW.YOURBOOKBONUS.COM
www.facebook.com/CarrieHartunianSmith

Chapter 4
A Succinct Message

Debbie is a number one best seller on Amazon, author of 'Social Media Fascination', and an active member in the Top Gun/Instant Customer Community. I had the honor of meeting Debbie Owen at my first live event. We spent quite a bit of time together talking about kids, education and her vision moving forward with her product. Debbie spent years as a high school librarian and now spends much of her time consulting with people about teaching and learning based on understanding how the human brain works best.

Since Debbie and I first met, her life and profession has changed considerably. After leaving the school system, she is now a full-time parenting expert and coach. She attributes much of this change to her Hot Seat back in February 2012.

The Hot Seat

Carrie: So, let me ask you this, when you were at the event what prompted you or why did you take what I consider a courageous step to fill out the Hot Seat application and get on stage; what were your hopes other than getting on stage?

Deborah: I am a semi-professional musician and I have been playing musical instruments and singing in various choirs and groups my whole life. So being on stage is not an issue for me. I was never nervous from that point of view. I always feel like the more exposure you can get for yourself and your business, the better.

I was hoping that I would get a few new ideas on how to get my message out and create my business, get it going and also be able to help people. So I was looking for one or two little things that I was not even thinking about yet.

Carrie: Great, Okay, so what suggestions might you have for someone who is wanting to stand out from the others to make sure that their application is seen; we know that those events are anywhere from three hundred plus I know the few times that I have gone back and looked into the basket where the Hot Seats are submitted –I do not know how many are in there but there is probably over a hundred. What suggestions might you have to help an application or you stand out to be selected.

Deborah: Well I will be perfectly honest, chatting up the host before the event is always a really useful thing. So I have made contacts with both Pam and Mike. You know I was in the VIP and had dinner with them and so honestly, that goes way back to when I was in college and I would go and talk to professors and hand things in early. I guess you could call me a brown-noser. But you know what I do not know if it is really that so much as looking for who are the influencers. That is a really important skill in business. It is part of networking. Who are the influencers? And so if you connect with whomever the influencers are in some way that is a really good thing that you can do. So that is the first thing.

And then the other thing is in terms of the actual application – the hot seat application itself – focus on the benefits: how do you anticipate helping your clients or your audience? Make it sound interesting like if you are another marketing executive you would better have something that is really unique about what you are offering because there are a million marketing people who are out there and so you need to come up with something that is interesting.

Carrie: You know those are great points. What I love about the first point is that Mike, and Ed and Pam, they are so accessible at the events for you to be able to catch their attention and introduce yourself to them. Whether it's in between sessions, prior to or after, seek them out and create a dialog with them, it really does work; go to every activity you can; and of course, finding what they are interested in and striking up conversation about that never hurts!

Deborah: Yeah that is right.

Carrie: I have been to several events and what I have noticed is that when I stand in the back of the room and I watch people who are contemplating the hot seat. I have noticed two different types of people, I have noticed those who I consider to be the ones who put their elbows up and kind of push their applications to the top, versus the ones who kind of are more timid, more reserved and need that extra encouragement. Do you have any advice for the person in need of that encouragement to just do it?

Deborah: Yeah I think that is exactly it; just do it. You never know by being on the stage and sharing your story how one little nugget might make a difference in your whole business. I remember at our events it was Paul who would usually just sit and listen to the other panelist who were kind of rattling things off, rattling things off, rattling things off and then most of the time, right at the end, Paul would come out with something that just totally changed the way the whole conversation went, and everybody was like; why were you sitting on that? So you just never know what somebody is going to say; and if you are an entrepreneur, you are going to have to be able to talk to people so just get over it; do it.

Carrie: And push forward; I like it.

Deborah: Get out of your comfort zone.

Carrie: So were there challenges for you once you got up on stage, and if there were, how do you overcome that?

Deborah: I think the biggest challenge is to express yourself succinctly; I remember there were a couple of people who were just going on and on and on, and I think everybody in the audience was starting to get a little antsy and that is when Mike would cut somebody off and say; okay let us just cut to the chase.

I had prepared significantly before I went up there, and we can talk about that in just a minute, but the thing was, the audience does not want a book, and neither does the panel, they want you to describe your product or your service quickly, get to the heart of whatever your problem or your issue might be. So trying to keep it clear but succinct is a challenge.

Carrie: I think that segues nicely into the next question. How do you prep for something like that?

Deborah: So I actually did prep for it, I put in my application and then once I found out that I was going to be picked sometime during the weekend and I did not know when; turned out I was in the very last on Sunday afternoon, but as soon as I found out I sat down and I wrote out a paragraph of exactly what I wanted to say and then I spent the next day and a half saying it over, and over, and over and over again.

So you have to practice and you have to prepare and make sure your message is clear and succinct.

I thought mine was pretty good, but it could have been even more succinct, because right as I was just about to finish my paragraph Mike cut me off.

Carrie: Did he cut you off with the questions or were you out of time?

Deborah: No, I think he cut me off as I was finishing my thoughts, so I just about made it to the end of my paragraph; that says to me that it was pretty good but it could have been even shorter.

Carrie: So is there one or two things that you can share; that was really the most impactful for you on stage?

Deborah: They asked if I had any testimonials to prove that my program works and as a newbie I had nothing. So since then I have been working to gather testimonials ever since, so that was certainly a key take away for me. Even if the testimonials that I am gathering are not specifically about this particular online course that I described at the hot seat; I am gathering testimonials about my services in general, and I am keeping a record. I have my new website that is coming up, and there are going to be a bunch of them on my website; so testimonials are absolutely critical for marketing. So my impactful moment was the embarrassing one, when I had no testimonials to verify or prove what I was claiming.

Carrie: That you are the expert that you are. Good, good, so how did you specifically benefit from your hot seat?

Deborah: Well first of all, clearly I need testimonials, so that is the first thing; but the major thing that they talked to me about was because I did not have any testimonials at that time, I need to run a beta version of my course and not try to have this like huge, enormous launch process that I am so used to seeing like through Jeff Walker's program or every time Frank Kern comes out with something or even when Mike or Pam come out with something.

What I really got out of my hot seat was you have got to have a beta launch. Have just a small group of people willing to step up at a low price and say, I am willing to give you feedback on how this is going and I know I will be getting in on the ground floor for a great price by doing that.

Carrie: So next time you head over to an event and you decide to get back on a hot seat; what, and this might fold back in to the tip question; but what one or two things will you pull from your first experience and make sure that you do different, in the next experience?

Deborah: What would I do differently?

Carrie: Yeah, so maybe a better way to say it, is if you could turn back the clock; what would be one or two things that you might do over?

Deborah: I would make my introduction a little bit shorter that would be the first thing. Otherwise I thought my hot seat went well, based on my product and what I was trying to accomplish at that time.

Carrie: If you were to provide one or two tips to someone who is either thinking about or definitely planning to fill out that hot seat form; what would you say to them to help them get the most out of their experience?

Deborah: So, clearly do not take up too much time on the front end, again it goes back to having your short introduction and then the really important thing, is describe the pain points that your product or service is trying to solve or address.

This is really important and it goes back to understanding what your big why is; whether it is the service or product you are providing or why you are an entrepreneur and what your business is in first place, or really almost anything in life, you will be far more motivated and much more effective, if you understand your big why.

So before you get up on stage be prepared to explain, at least to yourself and perhaps also to the panel and the audience; why is this important, what are the benefits to my customers and clients? The benefits, not the features, we keep hearing about that, not the features, the benefits. What is the pain point that your product or service is trying to solve? That is the really important thing.

Carrie: Yeah, great feedback, that will get you far on the panel and I think like you pointed out earlier, if you get that out early, then you have all that time to hear their feedback instead of fumbling around. Okay, so this is my favorite question, because I love to hear what everyone is up to, and what you are doing next. So I would love for you to tell us how things are going for you now, and how did that hot seat really transform your life, and your business?

Deborah: So that is a really good question, and because I was on the hot seat so early on in my decision to start this business, honestly I do not think it transformed my business, but it gave me a ton to think about.

So here I am still, five or six months later, I am working to implement the suggestions I have received during the hot seat. In fact I have pivoted my whole business slightly, as the feedback from that event, as well as a couple of subsequent events really helped me see that I was slightly off base in finding that sweet spot, where my own skills, talents and interests, meet the needs of the market; and that is really important, and I was off there.

So what I have discovered is that my sweet spot, is actually in parent coaching, not just in providing this one online course, to help parents help their kids learn better and faster, because that is what I started out with, because I had spent all these years as a teacher.

Yeah it is a great course, but it is not a business in and of itself, so my business is now parent coaching and the online course that I brought to that hot seat is one component of the whole business; and I do not think that they said that so much in their advice to me but because I was able to take what they taught, in terms of the testimonials and the beta course and talking to more people and I realize; okay I do not have a business, I have a one product and one product is not a business. So since that time, with that information, as well as I said information from some other places and other people that I have met along the way, I am creating this business of parent coaching and I am really excited about it.

Carrie: That is exciting; so you may or may not have come up with that coaching parent/coaching concept, had you not been on the hot seat.

Deborah: Well yeah, it was definitely part of being at that event for sure.

Carrie: great; and so tell, I would love to hear, what does that mean to be a parent coach; I am a parent and the thought of a parent coach is definitely an interesting concept, so what does that look like?

Deborah: So there is a lot of resources out there that talk about what we want our kids to be, we want them to be resourceful, we want them to be responsible, we want them to be respectful, we want them to have integrity; so those are all things that we want our kids to; kind of the end result of our kids and that is all really important and I would never take away from that. The problem is a lot of parents do not know how to get from where they are right now; which is often based on their own upbringing to helping their kids become those people that they want them to be; and so my business is focused around a three step process, which is basically how you; it is a servant leadership role in your family as the parent; and servant leadership; you know a lot of people think of leadership as power, it is not that at all it is the servant part; it is how you help the people that you are leading and serving grow and it is a perfect model for being a parent; and underneath that as well is emotional mass rebuild for yourself and for your children because how many kids fly off the handle; and how many parents then scream at their kids; there is this constant battleground going on; we need to understand how to control our emotions that way and it starts with the parents; and then the last component of that is also; so we have got serve with leadership, we have got emotional component and then we have also got the relationship component. So you have got the relationship with your child, you have got the relationship with your partner or your spouse; or the relationship with the teacher, and you look at the relationship between the child and the teacher. So all of these relational elements are key to being able to be a great parent as well; so those are the three pieces that I am focusing on; and what I do is I empower parents to become the best parents that they can be; so that they can coach their own kids to become the best adults that they can eventually be.

Carrie: Which we need so desperately in this day and age. So, how can parents find you? Give us your website and let us help change one family at a time.

Deborah: Yeah, terrific thank you. So my website is youcanraisegreatkids.com and my contact information is there; there is a contact page and you can write to me right through that contact page that is the way to do it. You can also find me on Facebook at Deborah C Owen; and I am also on twitter @DeborahCOwen; so you can contact me through any of those places and that is where I am most active.

Carrie: Great; and did I hear you say that you have another book on the horizon?

Deborah: Yeah I do; it is still untitled, but it is based around those three components, and hopefully by the time people are seeing this; the book will be available and you can get it for free on my website. I will also be posting it eventually as a kindle book on amazon. It is based around those three parts; servant leaderships, relationships, and emotional mastery.

Carrie: Well I really appreciate your time, and all of your great information about hot seats for people to really get up there and help transform their business. I look forward to checking back up with you in the future and see how your business is going.

Deborah: Awesome; thank you, you know what I just realized if people do want one of my books right now; you mentioned it at the top of our interview but, I have a book right now; it is about how parents can teach kids to use social media well; and it is called 'Social Media Fascination'.

Carrie: Great.

Deborah: So it is around a six piece model that I came up with; that no one else has come up with in terms of; how do we teach kids to use social media well; and in the process encourage them to be entrepreneurs and marketers themselves; which is kind of a cool way to look at it so.

To learn more about Debbie Owen visit
www.YouCanRaiseGreatKids.com

TO LEARN MORE ABOUT EACH OF OUR SUCCESSFUL HOT SEAT EXPERTS

VISIT
WWW.YOURBOOKBONUS.COM

SEE WHAT SPECIAL BONUS' ARE WAITING FOR YOU!

WWW.YOURBOOKBONUS.COM
www.facebook.com/CarrieHartunianSmith

34

Chapter 5
All The Way From Australia

If you've ever been around a Marketing Live Event in San Deigo CA, specifically an event with Mike Koenigs and/or Pam Hendrickson, you've probably either seen or have had the privilege of meeting Nobby Kleinman. He's best known in the community as the 'Cakes' guy! He loves his desserts.

Nobby shared that these live events is what brought him all the way from Australia to the states for the first time a little over 2 years ago and has been back five or six times since his first visit.

I first encountered Nobby on a Hot Seat in February 2014. I didn't get to actually meet him until late March, which is when I was able to spend time with this creative, dedicated and passionate Australian. Why would such a successful man desire an opportunity for a Hot Seat? I think you'll enjoy and learn some interesting concepts from Nobby's interview.

The Hot Seat

Carrie: Yeah, I lost count after about four or five... So you're definitely a veteran when it comes to their events and knowing hot seats. One of the questions I know that on the form that needs to be filled out with the hot seats is "Give me an interesting fact about yourself." Do you recall what your fun fact was?

Nobby: I think my fun fact was that I love traveling world, having coffee and cakes.

Carrie: Yes, and anyone who knows Nobby knows that you love your cakes; that's awesome. So for those people who are maybe looking at that form for the very first time, what suggestions might you have for someone wants to stand out from the crowd. How might you suggest someone make their hot seat form stand out from probably close to a hundred that are submitted?

Nobby: Yeah, absolutely, you do need to be different. It's not hard to do. Stop being shy. Be boastful about yourself. Say something that does make you stand out. So you've got to come out be outrageous.

I jump up and down on the desk; I don't care what you do. You are an individual, and that's what makes you different from everybody else. Tell people about who and what you are, what you do and why you are different. Be strong; you've got to be strong.

Carrie: Be strong, okay. So in general, what do you think the biggest challenge is for people once they get on stage on the hot seat?

Nobby: I would have said that it was initially overcoming stage fright, but the reality is that the team on stage actually makes you feel quite comfortable because they just start getting you engaged in conversation and take you through the whole process of beginning right in front of you, your website or your book or whatever it is. In general, it's a website. And for me, it was on one of my websites. So it's not hard; they'll take you through the process; they'll just lead you.

Carrie: You're so right, they're so great at making people feel at home and comfortable. Even when they're giving you that tough love.

Nobby: They definitely don't hold back, they do give you the hard and fast truth. While you might think that your site is beautiful and gorgeous to everybody, the guys are picking it apart. And as you said, it is tough love, and it's good stuff to get.

Carrie: And it's amazing how much value they can pack into the time you are up on stage – you're up there what 10-15 minutes?

Nobby: It seems like days.

Carrie: It seems like days, yeah, but they're able to really give you a lot of great implementable actions in such a short period of time.

Nobby: It doesn't matter how good you think you are, you can always do better, and it's people looking from the outside in, rather than you thinking about how beautiful your site is that can actually change everything.

Carrie: What or how do you think is the best way for someone to prepare themselves to get up on the hot seat? I've seen some people who at least appear to have prepped. And then there are those who go up there, and seems like they were putting together a business idea as they're walking up on stage. I don't necessarily think they are, but I don't think they've thought through what they hope to accomplish.

Nobby: I'd have to agree with you because I'm probably one of the second. I wasn't prepped. I ended up getting to the event, and I got to fill this form out for a hot seat, I didn't realize I suppose consciously what it was that I was filling out at the beginning until I realized that this was a possibility to get up on the stage.

For me, it was about one of my favorite things, which is leverage, and getting up on stage in front of a room of 300 people instead of trying to present yourself to 300 people on an individual basis, is great leverage. When I realized the value of that forum, I made sure that I put enough information on there to try to get to people and in front of the room. I think there was a number of factors, though, part of that novelty of being Australian in America and my friendship with a number of people and perhaps being a little bit different to a lot of other people. So there was a novelty that perhaps got me up on the stage as well.

Carrie: They sure love you Aussies.

Carrie: That's great. So okay, can you share one of the more impactful moments that you might have had while you were on stage?

Nobby: Yeah, when they kicked the crap out of my site. But can I tell you the tough love, which is what you called it before, did allow me to see that there were lots of opportunities for things I could be doing with my site. They just picked one of my sites, and it was to do with my book Want More Money, Honey? Which is a shameless plug. And I've implemented a number of things that the guys have said.

And so I took that on board and said, "These guys know what they're doing, what they talk about; they've been in this for a while, and they get around, and they've got access to people who do a lot of marketing; they know what they're talking."

Carrie: Good. So this might be a little bit redundant, but is there one specific thing that you benefited from the hot seat?

Nobby: Yeah. Well, like I said, I took on board what the guys said. I think the unfortunate part is that people think that it's just a bit of fun to get up in front of people. You do need to take advantage of whatever it is that you're told to do. These guys have got the experience. If you don't take on board what they say, you've just wasted an opportunity, and you've put yourself out in front of all the people, 300 people in the room .So you've exposed yourself.   So why the hell would you waste that opportunity.

Carrie: Yeah, good stuff, well said, good. So if you could turn that clock, that proverbial clock, is there one or two things that you'd like to do over?

Nobby: Yeah, I'd probably want to make sure that I completed the form a little more thoroughly to be sure that I got on stage. As I said, for me, what I do now with Outsource OK, being on the Hot Seat gave me an opportunity to be in front of a room of 300 people for them to know that I also did the outsourcing.

Although it happened in different hot seats, in fact, with Pam, and it wasn't so much a hot seat as much as I was a panelist. But once again, it put me out in front of a room of people who now found out that I did outsourcing.

So the hot seat with Mike, Paul and Ed focused on my financial book, helping women. But being asked to be on a panel in addition at that event allowed me to talk about my experience on outsourcing and, again, leveraged my position. So now with a proper team, I know about outsourcing, so am the go-to-guy; with a catalog available outside on the table.

Now I can put the two together and make that connection, and that's a very important thing. People come into our industry and buy all these programs; they still don't know what they need to do or who to go to. And all I keep hearing is go and outsource.

So whether you're there for a hot seat, or you're there for promoting, get out to the front of the room and make people know who you are at the moment.

Carrie: So you seized the moment, saw an opportunity and development a business basically from seeing a need in the community. What an interesting twist, you're up on stage for your book and then your outsourcing business grew from a different product, a book about smart financial planning. That's really a great story. So okay, next question, one of my favorites, if you were to provide one or two tips to someone who's either thinking about or definitely know they are going to fill out a hot seat application, what would you say to them to help them get the most out of their experience? What piece of advice would you provide in an effort to help either prepare for it or to get the most out of it once on stage?

Nobby: Okay. What you are doing right now is absolutely brilliant, because you are prepping them for when they get to be there and find that form on their seat because I had no idea, and I don't think everybody attending the event knew that those forms were going to be there. That form then goes up to the back of the room, and it's sifted through.

So you actually have to stand out. It comes back to what I said before, we all need to be outrageous, be courageous, be strong, be different, and stand apart from everybody else in the room. Why would they want to have you up in front of the room if you're the same as everyone else? You really want to be different.

Carrie: And it's great that you say that. What comes to mind when I hear you say that is – and I'm just going to add my tip now because it just came to me, but don't be afraid to go up and talk to Mike or Ed or Pam or Paul in between the meetings, so they get to associate a name with the face and tell them your story. They're great people, and they really want to hear yours – they're there to help everyone in that room, so not to be that flower child sitting in the back corner. So that I think goes hand in hand with what you said.

Awesome feedback, I know our readers are going to love it. But I want to make sure that we end our time together, hearing about you specifically, what you're doing and how things are moving along. You shared a little bit in the previous questions, but what's happening in Nobby's life and in your business, both as far as personally and/or professionally, that people who have been following you and have seen you on the hot seat would love to know or hear about?

Nobby: Okay. Well as I said, my passion is really around wanting to help women with money and also to be able to travel around the world to attend live events that I'm looking forward to going to and I've been invited to attend.

But the reality is most of my time is now spent in outsourcing. I'm helping a number of Philippine agents over here, and they're getting jobs.

Outsourcing OK is going to help a lot of people in the industry. We'll be that go-to company.

Carrie: Mike, Pam and Ed, are always telling people, "Don't do everything yourself. Do what you're best at, and outsource everything else." So to have someone in the community that understands the thought process is huge for what you are putting together.

What you were building originally for yourself, is now growing into something that all of us can benefit from. So that's just amazing, and it's great to see your business growing. And we'll make sure that we give a link to everyone in the book, so that they can seek you out; they'll see your face and know that you are the outsourcing king. That's what we need to do is crown you, The Outsourcing King.

Okay, well, Nobby, I've taken enough of your time. Thank you for valuable input on Hot Seats and look forward to seeing you at the next event.

Nobby: And I'll look forward to seeing you and everyone else there. Thanks Carrie. Bye.

To learn more about outsourcing visit www.OutsourceOk.com

TO LEARN MORE ABOUT
EACH OF OUR SUCCESSFUL
HOT SEAT EXPERTS

VISIT
WWW.YOURBOOKBONUS.COM

SEE WHAT SPECIAL BONUS' ARE
WAITING FOR YOU!

WWW.YOURBOOKBONUS.COM
www.facebook.com/CarrieHartunianSmith

Chapter 6
When Your Message Touches A Live Audience

I had the opportunity to meet with Pam Bartha, via Skype, to learn about her Hot Seat experience that she participated in back in February 2014, at the Instant Customer Live Event, in San Diego.

Pam has an amazing story! Clinically diagnosed with a debilitating illness in her 20's, she chose a non-prescription approach to therapy. Now more than 25 years later and still symptom free, she coaches others on the life-changing principles of wellness and prevention beyond pharmaceuticals. What a pleasure it was talking with Pam.

She is the author of **'Become a Wellness Champion'** and spends her time helping other on their journey to wellness.

The Hot Seat

Carrie: Well let me ask you this; what made you decide to do a hot seat; or what did you hope to get out of it?

Pam: Well I am extremely passionate about sharing the message that I bring in my book and in my coaching program, and so I look for every possible opportunity to get help from people that are very successful in the industry.

When I registered for their course or for the live event I should say, then we had the option of applying for a hot seat session and I saw it as an amazing opportunity to get feedback, to get insights from these incredibly, talented, gifted, successful people in this industry. They really understand how we need; what we need to do to get our message out to the world; and so any opportunity to pick their brains, and to get insights from them, I think is just incredibly valuable.

Carrie: That is great; I personally have yet to be on the hot seat; but I know the hot seat process is, fill out an application, submit it to the back of the room via the bin, and then wait to see if you get selected. Every time I walk back there and see the bin; there are tons of applications in there. Being these Live Events have a large crowd, maybe three to four hundred people; and you see the Hot Seat bin is over flowing with applications; did you do anything special to make yours stand out, to be selected?

Pam: Well I printed off the form; I think we got it before the event so I am sure that I printed it off before the event and I filled it out before the event; and then when I submitted it to the back of the room I just mentioned to the ladies back there, that I would really love to do it; it was really important to me; and then I did catch Ed as he was walking around and I was able to talk to him and just basically tell him that I would absolutely love to have a hot seat.

I really showed a desire and then in my forum I showed that I was really prepared for one.

That I was not just somebody just coming off the street; I had an idea; that I had already written a book, I had a website up and I had a message and I had a coaching program, so they had lots to work with. So I think being prepared; and it is not that you have to have to have all those things in place; but if you can be very clear also with your needs, I think that was another really important thing, is that if you can really be clear on what you would like help with; and whatever forum you are given, to really go through it and be very clear and meet all of their requirements; being prepared.

Carrie: So it sounds like, if you printed off the form beforehand, that you did a little bit of prep work.

Pam: Yes I did; I put a lot of thought in it.

Carrie: Good; so can you share maybe one or two tips; or one or two things that you did to be able to prepare; either prior to coming to the event and/or the day of the event?

Pam: I really did not do anything special; I printed off the form and they just had very specific sections that you had to fill out; so I just was as concise in filling those out and to the point and clear, and then also I am sure there was a section where they asked; why would you like a hot seat, what would you like help with?

I think really demonstrating that you are very serious about your business and that you have been putting effort in it is pretty easy for them to see how they can help you. I was very clear in laying out what I had, what I needed help with.

Carrie: Yeah; you know I have had some conversations with other people and that point; really keeps coming up time and time again. You only have fifteen maybe twenty minutes, if you are lucky, and if you spend fifteen of those minutes trying to explain what you do, then you only have five minutes to hear what they have say, so if you flip flop that around, try to get your message out within a few minutes, then you have that much more time to hear from them.

Pam: Yeah that is absolutely true.

Carrie: Good, okay, let me ask you this, in general; what do you think the biggest challenge is for people, once they get up on stage?

Pam: For most of us, it is the anxiety of being in front of a large group; and you know you are on a hot seat so you are not sure exactly what questions are going to ask and how you are going to answer it. But what really helps me is that if you are really passionate about what you do, that passion comes out really quickly and you just have to remember that. So sure, for the first few seconds you feel nervous but, I know with that group they're incredibly friendly and supportive. If you are able to get in that head space - focus on that, because then the fear goes away.

Carrie: Yeah, once you are up in the moment and you are talking about that.

Pam: That is right; or you can, if you have sometime maybe and if you are not used to being in front of a lot of people; maybe you can do a few meetings, or a few events of your own. Just talking to different groups; speaking to different groups, just so you feel a little bit more comfortable being in front of a larger crowd.

Carrie: I always say practice is a good thing, right.

Pam: Oh totally, but that is if you have enough notice, like with me it was; we just basically got the form and then we were off to the event within a day or two so.

Carrie: So that was a quick turnaround for you.

Pam: Oh yeah.

Carrie: Well I was at that event and I remember watching you up on the stage and I have to say that your message was very clear, very concise, and really a compelling product that you have; so it was really engaging. So let me ask you this; can you share one of the more impactful moments that you had while you were on stage?

Pam: Yes; in my marketing, because I work in the health field, my program can help everyone, but when you are starting off as somebody that the general public does not know; you cannot just reach the whole world. You have to narrow down your niche and I do know that and I have heard that over and over again, but it was really hard for me to figure out which niche to work with, and so when I was up there they told me, because I had overcome multiple sclerosis that, that would be the perfect niche for me to work in; but in my head I had it that most people that are dealing with multiple sclerosis, they are on disability and they cannot afford to pay me, so that; and I would like to do this all for free, but I have to pay my mortgage etc. So, that struggle within me, I do a lot of helping people for free, but I also have to be paid.

I have always avoided that niche, but they just kept hitting me with this like no you have to test out that market; and so since then I have been working in that market and I just finished a group of them just about a month ago, working strictly with MS, and I think that is a really great way for me to become well known and then from there other people take my program also because they understand. People are starting to get it; that wellness is not specific to; each person has different needs. We all have the same needs; we all basically have the same problems that we are dealing with on a fundamental basis so I think that, that has probably been my biggest obstacle is narrowing down my niche and figuring out where I want to start and I think for a lot of people that is the case. So they pointed me into the area that I really needed to go and which I was kind of avoiding;

which was good; which was really important.

Carrie: Well if I remember correctly, because you had such a compelling wow story, had MS and that makes your credibility that much more so, if I personally had MS, I am going to listen to you because you overcame it, but sometimes we get lost in our day to day business and we lose sight of the more basic approach. I think that is fabulous that, that came out on stage, it sounds like it changed how you were going about your business today.

Pam: It is so easy to talk to a smaller group than to try to hit a huge audience. When you are marketing you cannot talk to everybody and so when you talk to a smaller group it is so much easier to set up all of your materials, because you can narrow down what their needs are so much easier than if you are dealing with a huge wide variety of people that are kind of in a big group but not in the same narrow niche it makes like a lot easier to reach those people.

Carrie: Would you say that now you changed your marketing solely and specifically to hit that niche, or are you still doing what you were doing but just honed in on this market as well?

Pam: I have picked like three different markets and I have one coaching program that serves the three different markets. It is kind of the same as Mike's program, they have one marketing programs, so you do not change your message but when you are talking to different groups, when you are bringing them into your programs then you talk specifically to them.

So I am talking specifically to MS groups, Facebook groups and I will have a separate landing page for them and then bring them into the program. I will have a separate page for moms, etc. I have not started the moms group yet but that I think will separate because when you are dealing with kids versus adults it is quite different.

As far as people that are dealing with gut issues, all of those people can come into the same coaching program, but how you talk to them and reach them at first, is a little bit more specific to them; because they do not realize. It is just like when you attend Mike's events he is always saying we are all the same, it is all the same, whether you are selling vacuum cleaners or health or insurance. It is all the same business principles, marketing principles but you have to reach your audience specifically, because they do not know that at first.

Carrie: Let me just ask you this question. I always liked forward thinking but every now and again it is nice to take a look back and say; if you were to turn back the clock; is there one or two things that you might have done different; either in prepping or while you were on stage to really maximize your time that you had.

Pam: Well just the one thing that you mentioned is that if you only have twenty minutes that you want to try to make sure that you are as concise and clear, as quick as possible from the start. So mine was all right, but I would try to make it less about me and more about their insights and their advice. I think that, that is really something to keep in mind.

Carrie: Well we are getting to what I consider the crown jewel of the interview, and that is, if you were to provide one or two tips to someone who is either thinking about being up on a hot seat or has made up their mind; I am going to be on the hot seat I have got to get myself up there; what would you recommend to them to help them get the most out of their experience up there?

Pam: Being really prepared, being very clear with the message that you are bringing. Preparation, clarity and being as concise as you can and filling out the form. Knowing if they are allowing you to ask what you need; then to be very clear in what you need help with. But one thing that I wanted to mention as part of the benefits of being part of the hot seat; which I did not even anticipate this; and I did not even think about this but when I came down off of the stage I was swarmed by people for the next two days about wanting to connect with me, wanting to work with me and buying my book and taking my coaching program.

It is such an amazing opportunity, not just to get the incredibly valuable insights and advice from these experts, but then you literally have to put out the best business card you can for the whole . Whether it was people that had children, or nieces and nephews that were sick, that wanted help from me or just adults with all kinds of different health issues. So it is just such an incredible, huge blessing as far as promotion and making a connection so from that; one wonderful gentleman I connect with in Australia; and he has had me speak to his groups and people have registered and taken my program and we have developed an incredible friendship and working relationship; those kinds of things are just invaluable.

Carrie: So it sounds like getting yourself up on stage, to getting the information that you need to make the 2% shift Pam Hendrickson talks about is one thing, but the other piece is that your message gets out there to three hundred plus people; whoever is at this event. That is such a huge added benefit.

Pam: It is so much more than handing out a business card because they get to see you; they get to experience you, even just for a few minutes; so it is very powerful.

Carrie: So one more question for you; I would love to hear more about you, you shared a little bit in the previous questions; but I would love to hear more about what you are doing now. How the hot seat has transformed your life and your business?

Pam: I am the founder of 'Become a Wellness Champion', and I teach people how to reverse disease and how to stop disease symptom so that they can fully live their life. I work with people that thought they were really healthy but then; some of them just have symptoms; a lot of people that I deal with have chronic disease, so I teach them how they can take charge of their health. There are times when you have to work with health care professionals so but that way you can find the right one and you can reach your health goals much quicker; and so I used a holistic approach, but I really have an expertise in gut health; and when we take a lot of antibiotics; especially when we were children, way back then, it really threw the microbes that are in our GI track out of balance and overtime we end up with these silent, chronic infections in our body that, you do not get a high fever but you get all kinds of symptoms; it can start with fatigue and allergies and eczema and asthma or autoimmune disease and even cancer, so what I do is I bring people to a place where they really understand what it takes to be healthy and they pay attention to symptoms in their body and they get to choose the level of health that they want because they understand what it really takes to be healthy and how to reverse disease. So it is incredibly rewarding to help other people get their life back; because when I deal with chronically ill people a lot of them feel like their life has been stolen away from them and they are hopeless, there is nothing that they can do and that is so not true, and the cool thing is; is that what I have done there is more and more research coming out, supporting what I am saying, so it is not Pam's opinion I have so many resources of hero doctors; I call them, that are actually doing the same, and so I help people find those because sometimes they need to do tests, sometimes they need to use therapy so we still need to use our health care professionals, but to find the right one.

Carrie: Very powerful, I struggled with some medical issues a few years ago, and when I paid attention to what I was putting in your body, it is amazing, the changes that you feel. It seems so silly to say, but what you put in your body, impacts how your body works and it is crazy how quickly I felt the effects.

Pam: Oh, a hundred percent, and also one step further, is that the microbes' cells live in your body impact; so when you have the right microbes then you could handle that bite of pizza a little easier; when you have the bad microbes, then it; any bit of bad food, it feeds those microbes, they produce poisons and that makes you have pains, affects your head, fatigue. It is very important what you eat, but then equally important to be really working at building up that health. The best way to bring the good bacteria back is through the raw, live fermented vegetables; sauerkraut is more effective than any probiotic you would ever buy in the store.

Carrie: Nice little tip there. Well that is fabulous, I am going to have to reach out to you, and see how your coaching program can get me back on track; but Pam I really appreciate you taking the time to talk through your Hot Seat

Pam: It is such a pleasure for me.

Carrie: Okay, Pam, tells us how we can get a hold of you moving forward, for those people who might be reading this and are needing some guidance with their health issues, what is your website?

Pam: It is www.becomeawellnesschampion.com

To learn more about Pam Bartha visit
www.BecomeAWellnessChampion.com

TO LEARN MORE ABOUT
EACH OF OUR SUCCESSFUL
HOT SEAT EXPERTS

VISIT
WWW.YOURBOOKBONUS.COM

SEE WHAT SPECIAL BONUS' ARE
WAITING FOR YOU!

Chapter 7
From the Principal's Office To The Hot Seat

What an exciting interview; spending time with Jim House talking about Hot Seats just five short days after his book, Resetology™, Calming and Connecting Secrets from the Principals Office, hit #1 on Amazon in two categories, Parenting and Child Care. Not only do I completely respect Jim's techniques and unique parenting styles, I was flattered to work with him on his Best Seller launch of Restology™. We had quite a bit of fun working together and this interview continued the 'party' of working together!

With Jim being a regular around the Live Events Mike Koenigs/Pam Hendrickson plan each year, he definitely has watched the workings of many Hot Seats. He spent his time on the Hot Seat back in 2013 at the Author Expert Marketing Machines event.

The Hot Seat

Carrie: Okay, so let me ask you--why did you decide to do a hot seat, and what did you hope to get out of it once you got up there?

Jim: I'm a real student of continuous improvement. When I want to learn something new, I identify mentors that I trust and respect (trust is a big piece of this) I then pursue their teaching deeply and try to learn as much as I can. I knew that, as an audience member, I could derive really good value just from watching others get coached during the hot seats. However, I also knew that the take-aways would be far more powerful if I was the one being coached up there and getting specific suggestions for my new Resetology™ business from these experienced experts.

Carrie: As you were talking, it made me think of an analogy I use often, "Get in the game; you've got to get in the game." It's one thing to be sitting in the stands watching the game, spectator, versus being on the field and playing. Being on the hot seat, you're on the field playing for sure.

Jim: Yeah, no doubt.

Carrie: One of the things I love about the hot seat is that Mike is always encouraging people to keep things interesting. We are in show business, no matter our business. And he's always asking for interesting or engaging facts. Do you recall what your fun fact was, and why you selected it for the hot seat?

Jim: I'll talk a little bit about this later, but I filled out my hot seat application at home in advance. So I had a lot of time to think about this. He didn't actually ask me about my fun fact; he started off with, "Tell us a story ..." But on the application I put lover of milkshakes, and I also talked a little bit about singing in barbershop quartets. I tried to write things that were fun and really unique, and that may have captured their attention, but they didn't actually ask me about that from the stage.

Carrie: So let me ask you this, what suggestions might you have for someone who wants to stand out from others when they're filling out their application?

Jim: The whole process of transforming from an educator to an entrepreneur has challenged me to identify the essence of who I am--what are the things that make me unique? What are the things that juice me and get me excited to get out of bed in the morning? That honest, pure uniqueness is what I tried to convey.

Carrie: So there are 300+ people that go to an event. I don't know how many hot seat applications are filled out, but I know I've gone to the back of the room, and catch a glimpse of the little bin holding all the applications, which are over flowing from the basket.

Jim: It's definitely overflowing.

Carrie: So how do you stand out from all the rest in that process to make sure that you are selected? I'm assuming everyone who fills out a form hopes to actually get up on stage.

Jim: You asked me to give you some tips, and I'm going to jump ahead and give you one right now-- I already alluded to the fact that I filled out my hot seat application in advance at home. I don't know if they still do this, but after I paid for the conference, I received an email that had all the hotel information, and it also had a hot seat application attached as a PDF.

So I opened up a Word document on my laptop and just started brainstorming answers to each question. I had the time to revise my ideas and present them in a clear fashion.

For me, that was really helpful. I knew it would work to my advantage if I demonstrated that I had my act together. I would not have been able to convey that level of preparedness if I had filled out the application while at the event.

Carrie: That's great feedback. You're the first person that I've heard that has done it prior to getting there. And so for those people, who are serious and really want to get up on stage, take the time and fill it out beforehand. I like it.

Jim: I actually printed it out, too. So mine was the only one in the pile that was not hand written.

Carrie: Okay, I think that's a nugget right there because that's going to differentiate your application from anything else.

Jim: And I did a tiny bit of desktop publishing, I put my logo on the top, and formatted the document a little bit to make it pop.

Carrie: Wow, you definitely went the extra mile to leave an impression; that's fabulous. Thanks for sharing that tip. It's the first time I've heard anyone mention that. So let me ask you this, in general, what do you think the biggest challenge is for people, once they get up on stage, and they're live with their hot seat?

Jim: I'm going to give you another peek at how I usually prepare. I spent a lot of time thinking about what I wanted to say, and I had intended to rehearse answering the questions beforehand. I also paid attention to the questions the panel asked during those hot seats who went before me and formulated some quick answers to those questions, too. Right off the bat, Mike asked me a question that he had not asked anyone else before me. He said, "Tell us a story about a time when Resetology™ impacted someone's life." Fortunately, a story came right to mind. And it was a fun story; it was the right story.

So, in terms of a challenge, I would say some folks have not thought through what they want to say, and it looks like they're struggling to figure out what they want to say, and how they want to say it.

And then I think nervousness affects all of us at different levels.

Carrie: Yeah. Any suggestions on how to overcome that?

Jim: How to overcome it? Preparation for me is my go-to – anytime I'm presenting anything, I want to have an answer for every kind of question that's going to come up. Not memorized, just prepared.

Carrie: I think that being prepared is huge. And the reality is I think no matter if you're the person who's gung-ho to get up there or you're the timid person, our bodies react, and you're going to have some nerves. And so at the risk of sounding really heartless, I'd say, "Suck it up and do it."

Jim: That's the entrepreneur's life right there, isn't it?

Carrie: Yes it is! So my next question kind of might be a little redundant based on what we've talked about, but maybe you have one or two tips here. What or how do you think is the best way to prep for the hot seat? You did a lot of prep beforehand. Do you have one or two things that can help someone who's maybe not a prep person?

Jim: Another one I have is a visual image tip. You sit in a tall director's chair up on stage, which most of us are probably not used to sitting in unless you are a famous movie director.

I've seen people lean back and look really uncomfortable. So, I would suggest you go up on stage during a break and get comfortable sitting with good posture in the chair ahead of time.

Those silly captain's chairs that are uncomfortable and unruly with high armrests and these oddly positioned footrests. I know this may sound insignificant, but I think if you are physically feeling centered, it's easier to be present and it's easier have a better interview.

Carrie: That's a great tip that you just put out there that I would have never thought of, but those chairs are clumsy to get in and out of. And if you're a female, and you're wearing a skirt, how do you sit? And yeah, it's something to think about, good. I appreciate you bringing that up. So how did you specifically benefit from your hot seat?

Jim: In a lot of ways. In case I forget, remind me to tell you about the people that I met because of the hot seat. With Resetology™, I make life easier for busy parents by equipping them with the confidence and ability to quickly calm kids, transform irritating moods and connect in the fun ways that they've always longed for.

I have been training parents in workshops and as individual clients for about three years, but I was an educator first and entrepreneur second. I've had to change my whole mindset and learn a whole new repertoire of skills to become an entrepreneur.

I already knew with absolute certainty (I had loads of social proof) that I was helping lots of families to be better connected and to have less stress and have more fun.

I really wanted to help families on ambitious scale, but after the first year I began to think, "Okay, God, if I'm just supposed to train only a hundred people a year, so be it--this is my life's mission, and this is how I'm gifted to help people. So we'll just train a hundred parents a year, and I'll figure out how I'm going to make enough money to live." I really wanted to pursue the bigger vision, but I wasn't sure if this idea was that scalable.

When I got up on the stage though, Pam Hendrickson was amazingly affirming about it. She said, "I love what you're doing. You have so much credibility. The world needs more of this--this is great! It's just a traffic problem"

Pam has unparalleled experience in creating and bringing all sorts of powerful information products to market. But what I love most about Pam is that she talks about her kids all the time! So, when she was so enthusiastic, I knew in that instant that this mission could be bigger-- I just needed to figure out how. I went from having a small mindset of "We'll help as many people as we can" to "We can go out to the world with this."

Everyone on the panel had excellent tactical suggestions for me about how I could move forward in my business--they were great! And Pam's enthusiasm impacted me on a deeper level, too.

Carrie: I'd like to say you never would have received that if you weren't up on the hot seat. So you can directly attribute that empowerment to the stage, to the hot seat.

Jim: Hundred percent correct, absolutely.

Carrie: You were going to tell me about people you met.

Jim: Thank you! When I finished the hot seat, I walked off the stage toward the back of the room. Along the way, I was stopped four or five times by people who wanted to interview me, wanted to collaborate with me, or wanted to connect me with someone else.

And so immediately, I've got these new relationships. I had been exchanging business cards all weekend long, but now people wanted to engage – they were coming to me and engaging with a specific reason.

And then I was in the back of the room, and this one young woman came up, literally running across the room in this very colorful dress – I didn't know her – and said, "Oh, my gosh, we have to work together! Our work is so complimentary!" She has become a wonderful friend.

So the hot seat also gave me exposure to 300 people in the room, and while there is such incredible content at these events, for me, the even bigger take-has been the incredible relationships that I've developed--both entrepreneurial and social.

Carrie: So I'm just going to connect the dots here real quick. It sounds like your biggest benefit from being up on stage was Pam's enthusiasm which really helped elevate your certainty to the level that you wanted to be--that's fabulous.

And then I think all too often what can happen is after the event you go home, and you get back into the day-to-day mire of "What am I doing" and possibly losing your purpose and the vision. But then when you meet these people who saw what they saw up on stage, then you have those people to help carry you through. So that's cool how I think God just places those people in our life to help carry that vision through. So cool.

Jim: Amen.

Carrie: Great. Okay, we have a few more questions. I love talking through this with you; it's been fabulous. I hate to look at my past , the whole coulda, woulda, shoulda bit, but I equate it to when you are on a road trip, there are times you need to look in the rear view mirror. There is value in it just to see what you just came through, the progress you are making.

So if you were to turn back the clock, would there be one or two things that you would have done differently either getting up on stage or once you were on stage? And you can say no.

Jim: [Big thinking pause] I'm not avoiding the question . . .

Jim: I honestly can't think of something that – I mean it wasn't perfect, but I didn't have a moment of regret, "Oh, I wish I had done that."

Carrie: And I would say because you prepared so darn well, it sounds like. So that's a good point right there. Okay, so I know you've already provided a couple, so I'm just going to ask the question, and let's see what resonates here.

If you were to provide one or two tips to someone who's either thinking about or definitely planning to fill out that hot seat form, what would you say to them that would help them get the most out of this experience? Maybe what piece of advice would you provide in an effort to help them prepare to get the most out of it?

Jim: Here are a couple of little things that I would do before you go up – because they do tell you in advance that you're going up. They won't surprise you. At least they did not surprise me.

Have someone take notes for you while you're up there. You may get access to the video afterward, but that will take awhile. I actually took my journal up on stage with me, and I took notes. I think I'm the only I have ever seen do that. But if I don't write it down, it's gone. So I had my journal with me. And while they were talking, I was trying to look at them, and take notes, as well.

Another small tip along that line, is that you're up there on stage with some of the most recognized leaders in the industry. So it's a nice photo opportunity, as well. So I would dress accordingly. I've used these photos on my website and in social media, and that's valuable.

Carrie: So I had a question while you were talking. I'm familiar with the hot seat selection process--fill out the application, submit it, do something out of the ordinary to be selected. But what's the process after that? Do they call you? How do you know you're going to be on stage? And how much time do you have from the time that they tell you till the time you go on stage?

Jim: So, at the end of the session right before lunch on the first day, Jessie came out front, and said on the mic, "Okay, we need…" and there was a litany of names, "we need Carrie Smith, Jim House, Verlinda Thompson, please come up to the front right now. I need to see you before you go to lunch." We gathered up front by the stage and Jessie gave us a quick overview of the process.

Carrie: So if you hand in your application on Friday, and you're not on until Sunday or whatever day, you don't know until a couple hours before.

Jim: So at the event I was selected, they named all of the hot-seat participants all at once on the first day. But they may have received some really interesting hot-seat applications later during the event. Here are a couple of little things that I would do before you go up – because they do tell you in advance that you're going up. They won't surprise you. At least they did not surprise me.

Have someone take notes for you while you're up there. You may get access to the video afterward, but that will take awhile. I actually took my journal up on stage with me, and I took notes. I think I'm the only I have ever seen do that. But if I don't write it down, it's gone. So I had my journal with me. And while they were talking, I was trying to look at them, and take notes, as well.

Another small tip along that line, is that you're up there on stage with some of the most recognized leaders in the industry. So it's a nice photo opportunity, as well. So I would dress accordingly.

I've used these photos on my website and in social media, and that's valuable.

Carrie: So I had a question while you were talking. I'm familiar with the hot seat selection process--fill out the application, submit it, do something out of the ordinary to be selected. But what's the process after that? Do they call you? How do you know you're going to be on stage? And how much time do you have from the time that they tell you till the time you go on stage?

Jim: So, at the end of the session right before lunch on the first day, Jessie came out front, and said on the mic, "Okay, we need..." and there was a litany of names, "we need Carrie Smith, Jim House, Verlinda Thompson, please come up to the front right now. I need to see you before you go to lunch." We gathered up front by the stage and Jessie gave us a quick overview of the process.

Carrie: So if you hand in your application on Friday, and you're not on until Sunday or whatever day, you don't know until a couple hours before.

Jim: I've heard of a couple of stories like that.

Carrie: Okay.

Jim: So at the event I was selected, they named all of the hot-seat participants all at once on the first day. But they may have received some really interesting hot-seat applications later during the event.

launched this. And if you haven't gotten your copy of the book, yet, you need to check it out-- it's fabulous read, and it's an easy read, too. That's what I like about it.

Jim: Thank you very much, very kind.

Carrie: Well, thank you so much, Jim. I appreciate your time, and we look forward to seeing you in the future and to watching you grow your business to help more families.

Jim: Likewise, I look forward to reading your book, as well! And I'm excited for your future clients who are smart enough to hire you like I did! Thanks, Carrie!

To learn more about Jim House and Resetology™ visit
www.Resetology.com

Chapter 8
Gratitude

I had the opportunity to meet with Delina Farjardo, via Skype, to learn about her Hot Seat experience which she participated in back in October 2013. The Rocktober Fest Live Event, in San Diego.

What a calming spirit Delina has. Her Hot Seat perspective is definitely one to review. Having a very interesting background combination, trained and practicing challenging levels of medicine as a physician's assistant, as well as a Certified Life Coach with Anthony Robbins, she brings a different perspective to maximizing your time on the Hot Seat.

The Hot Seat

Carrie: So let me ask you this; what prompted you to take the steps to do a hot seat; what was the hope or the outcome you were looking for?

Delina: I think I wanted to experience the hot seat, but not from the perspective of how I look at me; more of, I need to learn how to get outside of my comfort zone with public speaking, and why not do it in a setting that was supportive, and I felt very supported with Mike Koenigs. He had spoken to my group in the past and I felt a strong connection and I thought this was a great way to start to share myself and my distinctions; and start to break through some of the beliefs that I had about being in such an environment like a hot seat, or on stage.

Carrie: Nice; yeah I will say that, that whole group [Mike Koenigs, Ed Rush, Pam Hendrickson and Paul Colligan], they are so nurturing and comfortable to be around. If you are ever going to do something like that, step outside your comfort zone having that group of people sitting next to you, I think is; for me comforting; they are just so relatable and kind.

Carrie: Did you do anything special to make you and or your application stand out?

Delina : No, I did not do anything special, I filled out the same application in the same way that everybody else did, I think that maybe the details that I put in my application might have made the difference. I felt like maybe Mike or the panel resonated with and thought yes she is very congruent with that; and so we would like to get her on stage.

Carrie: Yeah, and that is really important, I know that they definitely concentrate on that sort of thing. Great, okay; so before you got there, did you do any kind of prep work, to get yourself ready to do a hot seat?

Delina : It is interesting because, that hot seat, I did not even know what I was stepping into and that is how much my outcome was stepping outside of my comfort zone. So I had no idea what the rules or, what they were looking for, or what needed to; or how to prepare for something like that. I believe as I saw the hot seat people go up I realized there was actually a protocol that I was supposed to be following; but I did not know. So I did not prepare; we had a lunch break prior and people were asking me, aren't you going to; and I go no; I am just going to stand up as I am; like what am I supposed to do.

I saw another person that went on the hot spot; and she was sitting with her boyfriend and she was writing and they were practicing and she was rehearsing and that was making me more nervous actually. She was going through questions and rehearsing the hot seat interview I guess, and looking on actually made me more nervous, because I knew how I wanted to show up so my only preparation was I had lunch with my group of coaches and friends, and then afterwards, before I went on to the hot seat, I went back to my hotel room just to kind of find that alignment and to get back into that space that had the courage and the strength and the trust to get up there, I had nothing mentally prepared for that.

Carrie: The way you prepared yourself; getting one with yourself, is a much different approach from what I have heard up to this point, and I think it will definitely resonate with certain readers. Having been a recent 'student' of watching a lot of hot seats, I have seen that depending upon where you are in the 'line up', if you are the first, second, third and which day, kind of depends on how the format changes so, if you are one of those people who plans to a T, and then get up there and they throw you a curve ball that could really throw someone for a loop.

Delina: Because I was not prepared for some of the questions, I had my own learning experience up there for sure. I understood what the experience was while I was up there, I understood the higher purpose, and I think the panel did too. So it was not about me delivering from a mental place is was about me making a breakthrough and connecting with the audience.

Carrie: Okay so when you were up on stage and you were sharing your business was there one or two things that were an impactful moment for you; whether it was someone gave you an idea, or they shared a mind shift; what was the most impactful thing?

Delina: Sure; Pam had mentioned, I am a Tony Robbins coach, we learn a lot of language or what she calls jargon that becomes embedded in us that we think in that language. What I learned most is to be mindful not to use jargon, as the audience does not come from that background necessarily.

So then Mike had asked everybody to raise their hands if they understood what I was talking about, half . That is my whole purpose and my whole niche is about that; so I was on stage as a coach, saying that I really help people get through that; I help people with their identity and I help people find their true purpose in life; and I know from my perspective from my story, that you cannot stack achievements because once you get to the finished line you will still find that you are unfulfilled and that is being unsuccessful. So Pam had mentioned that you have to remove the jargon and you have to explain it in laymen's term so Mike asked the question how many people understood what Delina was talking about, when I said it the first time, half the room raised their hands because they didn't understand that jargon; they are in the industry too, but more people would understand if I kind of just broke it down to them and simplified and explained what I meant.

The other thing that was a big point for me, my take away, was my story, my biggest choke hold on myself; was I did not want to reveal myself; I did not want to reveal my story, it was uncomfortable being on stage, really letting people in to know me. Mike said, Delina, the people want to connect with you - not with the jargon.

Carrie: That is good stuff; I am taking notes as you were talking and it is so true because, when you tap into it; and I'm sure you see this as a coach when you talk to someone, but when you tap into their core it just opens them up so much more to where they can receive what you have to offer so much easier.

Delina: The real breakthrough for me was being on stage and not coming from a place of "okay now I have to perform" and that was huge for me, because stepping out of my comfort zone and being on stage period, that is the first time I have ever been on stage, the first time I have ever been in a hot seat, that was the first time I have ever spoken publicly to people in a group like that setting.

Carrie: Well there is such a huge vulnerability if you truly take advantage of what is being offered on the stage.

Delina: I really pushed myself to the edges of my comfort and a lot of that is not watching people in the hot seat; so I did not walk in until like five seconds before I was called out to go on stage, they were actually waiting for me.

Carrie: that is a great point; and that is going to lead us into the next part I think. That is a good tip. If you are wired like you are, that sitting there and listening to other people could absolutely impact your time on stage.

Delina: Absolutely. All of a sudden you are thinking I am not good enough. I am not good enough! Or, she said that, what if they want that, maybe I should start changing what I am going to say... So I walk on stage with just my truth, I had no idea what I was going to be asked; I had no idea what the format was; again I did not follow the rules very well.

Carrie: If you were to provide one or two tips to someone who was either thinking about or definitely saying yes I am going there to try and get on a hot seat what would you tell them that could help get the most out of their experience/situation?

Delina: I guess the feeling that I keep having when you ask that question is what is their intention? To go there and get in the hot seat? Because that was not my intention. You will not get in the hot seat if that is your only intention. So that is one.

Delina: when I was in the hot seat people could see that my responses were different. Like I was getting people coming up to me as I walked off stage and were coming/getting out of their seats to say thank you without me even going to the back of the room yet. The response I was getting from the people in the audience was different because of that energy. They could feel my vulnerability. They could feel that this was coming from a different place. It was not another sales pitch

Carrie: it was real and raw and true – sounds like. Absolutely.

Delina: raw and true. It was about getting the help that I needed to help you. It was about that panel of people. It was about being at the right place at the right time and about the panel of people recognizing I guess my message and a servant's heart and vulnerability and rawness and congruency and then say hey this could be a great person to put on stage because people who resonate with this maybe they will see their truth in it or maybe they will see that is much more enlightening.

Carrie: Absolutely.

Delina : I'd also say trust in your message. That would be the second one. And the third one I would say is self-love and acceptance. Because of your message you have to have self-love and acceptance. Trust your message have some clarity; you know a lot of people who ramble; have some clarity. Put trust in your message and also trust in your flow. Do not stick to a script because you will miss the whole thing. Trust in your flow and have gratitude. Even if you do not get picked be grateful. I was so grateful to be there. I was so happy. I was coming from a whole different vibration that is just the truth you know.

Carrie: I am highlighting the gratitude. In all the interviews I have done on Hot Seats, I've heard many great things, but the gratitude piece is so important. Mike, Pam, Ed are completely interested in helping others and they do not have to be. They have their products that they are selling but they are really invested in everyone that they meet and talk to some degree. To have gratitude towards them, I think does wonders for everybody. It keeps the energy flowing in a positive direction.

Delina: I did not give them a business card I did not give them a book I did not have anything extra only that maybe I was vibrating from gratitude. And when your energy is picked up all over the place you can see that you know and maybe that came through. And so yes gratitude! Have a lot of gratitude even if you do not get accepted on the hot seat. Be grateful about that too.

Carrie: That is a fabulous life lesson for everything in your life, fabulous, just fabulous. So in closing I would love for you to tell us a little bit about how that hot seat transformed you, your life, your business. Give yourself a plug, tell us how to get in touch with you, what you are doing now, and a little about you.

Delina: I am a life and a business coach and I have published three books since the hot seat.

Carrie: Wow! Three books!

Delina: All three books were best sellers on Amazon and they are titled a series "Purpose Now." Our readers can go to my website and take a free quiz! It'll help people find out if they are truly living their passions and purpose in life.

Once you finish the quick questions it will put you in a group of four different profiles. You will get a free report based on your profile and then hopefully we can take that quiz to the next level and I can help you through the coaching program.

Carrie: Great. Thank you so much for your time and giving us some really insightful tips to think about before entering into the Hot Seat forum. This feedback will bring calmness to certain people who are looking for Hot Seat guidance. The more peace people have as they are walking through this part of their journey the more clarity they will have on stage. You bring a dynamic that has not shown up yet! Thank You.

To learn more about Delina Fajardo visit
www.DelinaFajardo.com

TO LEARN MORE ABOUT
EACH OF OUR SUCCESSFUL
HOT SEAT EXPERTS

VISIT
WWW.YOURBOOKBONUS.COM

SEE WHAT SPECIAL BONUS' ARE
WAITING FOR YOU!

Chapter 9
Rock Star!

When you hear the words 'Rock Star,' you might think about your favorite Rock-N-Roll band from the 60's, 70's or 80's or someone regularly in the public eye. Ever since February 2014, when I hear the words *Rock Star*, I think of Andy Falco Jimenez.

We met at Mike Koenigs Live Event. Seeing Andy on stage as a panelist and spending time with him in the preceding months Certifications and Live Events, I knew he had accomplished amazing things in a short period of time, however I had no idea how much he accomplished, in that period of time, until I had the privilege of hearing a recap of his Hot Seat in August 2014 at another Mike Koenigs Master Class special event.

I was not at the event when Andy first came on stage, but Mike describes him as walking on stage as a broken man. In this chapter, I'm going to give you the Quentin Tarantino version first, so keep reading to see Andy's Hot Seat unfold, during an event in August 2014, 18+ months after his original time on stage.

August 2014, Mike Koenigs Master Class: Andy's Interview Mike

I was broke and in debt, my house was in foreclosure, I had a need and a desire to figure my way out, I just had to do it, a Traffic Geyser staff member made it possible for me to attend the event, I got on a Hot Seat and told my story of where I was and where I was hoping I could go. I talked about my police dog training, my pet dog training, shared a book idea I had, the panel was brutally honest at my lowest moment which is exactly what I needed to hear. I took your [Mike Koenig] advice and at first only did part of what you [Mike] suggested and had some success. I learned my lesson and then followed all of what you [Mike] told me to do. I was able to get my house out of foreclosure, began to pay off my bills, became debt free, AND just recently landed a contract with the Kingdom of Bahrain for $350K.

I was a police officer for 24 years. I was strong willed, very manly… I thought I had everything, houses, cars, we were doing really well. When I lost the material things it took everything out of me. To share, on the stage, what I was I was going through was not easy.

I just knew that I hit the bottom. I have five children, some of them very young. I love them dearly. And to think … I had to sleep in my car at the event. I couldn't afford a hotel room. I couldn't afford the gas. I had to borrow money to get from Orange County to San Diego.

It's a pretty terrible place to be, when you begin to think, 'I'm sleeping in my car now - Am I going to have to find a way to sleep in this car with my family?' They had relied on me and I felt I had let them down. There had to be no other options, I would not accept failure. I realized that Mike and his team is where I was going to hang my hat.

Everything you [Mike] have said to follow and when I follow it, it works. I had written a book and didn't follow the system and didn't go to number 1. I wrote another book, followed your systems and went to #1. Everything that I have currently I owe to God, and the Hot Seat panelist, and I appreciate it.

I had the pleasure of sitting next to Andy while he shared his story about his Hot Seat. I later caught up with him to ask him some questions behind his time on the original Hot Seat.

Interview with Andy after his Hot Seat

Carrie: Let me ask you a couple of questions about your original Hot Seat. What made you feel compelled to get on the hot seat? What did you hope for when you went on to your hot seat?

Andy: Interestingly enough, when I went to the event there in San Diego for the first time, I didn't know what to expect. I didn't know what a hot seat was and but they said that if you have a business, you may want to apply to be on one of our hot seats.

If I was going to be there, if I dragged myself there with nothing in my pockets, slept in my car, because I couldn't afford to get a hotel -- I should at least go for everything. I should be trying to get a hot seat to get these experts to help me figure out what I was missing. And see if the marketing they would teach, would help me work through what needed to be done, so that I could survive, I could keep my business and didn't have to work for Starbucks as a Barista.

Carrie: Nothing wrong with that, right?

Andy: Yes. Nothing wrong with that, but that is not what my goal for my life was. I really wanted to do something with my life. To be able to help people as an expert and be successful in it. So, I fill out the application. My whole goal at that point was to be on that hot seat and just to get basically torn apart or something. To just allow the panel to open me up and teach me all the things that I was thinking the wrong way about. I was ready for it, prepared. I truly know that for some reason, that is what I needed to do, I need to be on that hot seat.

Carrie: It sounds like you are highly motivated to get yourself up there. How or why do you think you were chosen out of all the applications?

Andy: There was one thing on there that said, tell us something funny about yourself or interesting about yourself. My wife, she is 20 years younger than I am. So thought if I put it on there that I am an old guy with a young wife, struggling to make his business work and have three mouths to feed at that time that it might catch their eye.

So, I brought up the point that I was an older guy with a younger wife. I forgot what I wrote exactly, but it was something that really drew attention. I had everything else figured out, except for how to market my business.

Carrie: Well, it sounds like it did, because you got on the stage. Let me ask you this. A few minutes ago you mentioned something about preparing for it. What did that look like for you? How did you prepare?

Andy: I had no idea what I was going to expect. I wish I would have prepared. I think the only preparation I did was mentally prepare myself to be torn apart, because they already had a couple of hot seats before that and I began to see what they did. I mentally prepared. I want them to find everything that needed to be fixed. I wanted to to be able to take it as constructive criticism and not be defensive and close-minded. That was the biggest thing. They flat out told me that I was not marketing to my market. That I was marketing to myself. I did not want to believe that. I designed my website. I love my website. I love the name of the book that I was trying to write at the time. They said, you are in love with your title, but your title is not directed for your market. It is directed for people like you and you are not your market. Your market is something completely different.

You may have a website visitor named Mary, a seventy-five year old dog owner who is having problems house training her dog, or maybe her dog is jumping on neighbor's kid. If she goes to your website, she is going to be repelled from your website. As a matter of fact, she is not even going to click on your website.

And that was one of the first things that they told me. They told me the title of my book sucked. That was awesome because that was exactly what I needed to hear.

Carrie: It sounds like they gave you some tough love.

Andy: I knew I had to be prepared to hear it. As far as being prepared, that was the only thing that I was prepared for. You have to be open to it and then accept it. Thank God I did and made those changes, because once I did, everything changed. I began to be far more successful.

Carrie: You might have already answered this question, but I am just going to throw it out there. Is there one thing that was really impactful for you on stage, like while you were sitting there, it hit you like a ton of bricks?

Andy: Yes. The thing was that I didn't know my market. At this point, I have been running my dog training business for about twenty years. For them to tell me that for twenty years, I have not been marketing to my market, was a little shocking. I go, really? I've spent years of marketing my business the way that I thought I was supposed to and it was completely wrong!

Carrie: That is definitely interesting. Okay, just one more question, if you were to provide one or two tips to someone who was either thinking about or definitely planning to try to get up on stage for a hot seat, what would you say to them to really get the most out of their experience?

Andy: In your application, make sure that whatever that particular event is discussing, whether it is Facebook marketing or YouTube, Livecasting or writing a book. Whatever it is, make sure your application has that in mind, does that make sense?

Carrie: Yes, So if the event segment is about doing a podcast...

Andy: If you want to get up on the hot seat and the whole theme for that event is podcasting, your application should include an element of 'podcasting' into the applications – like 'I want to figure out how I can implement a podcast for our business.' Second, just think of something that is unique to you and that makes your story stand out. Everybody has a story and that is the power.

Carrie: Mike is always about, give me something interesting. Give me something engaging. He wants good content. So, if you have a good story, he is going to see value in that.

Note from Carrie

Not only has Andy turned his own business around, but he now consults with businesses, outside of dog training, helping them to grow their business. He has created a podcast, *Fearlessly Successful,* to help those feeling stuck in life to break through the fears that come with your journey to success. Check it out on iTunes.

https://itunes.apple.com/us/podcast/to-succeed-you-must-start/id877001188?i=317315830&mt=2

To learn more about Andy Falco Jimenez visit
www.FalcoK9Academy.com

**TO LEARN MORE ABOUT
EACH OF OUR SUCCESSFUL
HOT SEAT EXPERTS**

**VISIT
WWW.YOURBOOKBONUS.COM**

**SEE WHAT SPECIAL BONUS' ARE
WAITING FOR YOU!**

WWW.YOURBOOKBONUS.COM
www.facebook.com/CarrieHartunianSmith

Chapter 10
The Lost Transcript

Within the first few moments of speaking with Blair Barnhardt, his personality shines through. I first 'met' Blair while he was on his Hot Seat at the February 2014 Live Event. As mentioned in a previous chapter, having interviewed several experts for this book there were a few people I really wanted the opportunity to connect further with, Blair was one of them.

Blair is an award winning National Highway Institute Instructor, serial entrepreneur, filmmaker, musician, speaker and Founder/Executive Director of the International Pavement Management Association. Over the last twenty years, he has designed and delivered green, cost-saving pavement management, in-place asphalt recycling and preservation programs across North America. His Three-Legged Stool System of pavement management forms the basis for most all of the curriculum he teaches in the Book on Better Roads.

I was crushed when the transcript files from our interview turned up corrupted and I only had my handwritten notes as evidence of the amazing interview I had with Blair. Although this chapter cannot ever include the entire depth of our conversation, I wanted to be sure to share some of the highlights of our time together.

When asked about why he chose to apply and participate in the Hot Seat, Blair provided the classic entrepreneur response, "When you are in a room with 300+ people, to reach as many people as you can, there's only one way ... to be on stage."

He attributes his comfort level of being on stage to his years of performing with a band. Although, Blair admits, the moment right before he steps on stage he still gets a nervous feeling. But he wants beginners to know, "You wouldn't be normal if you didn't get that nervous feeling!"

What I found extremely interesting was Blair's advice for how to prepare to take the Hot Seat:

'There wasn't not much 'prep' before being notified that I'd have a Hot Seat slot," he began. His thought process was that participants should be prepared each day for the opportunity to be on stage. Regardless of whether there is a Hot Seat vacancy or not.

'Being on stage' also includes meetings with potential clients, bankers, joint venture partners. It means showing up prepared to take the stage during mastermind groups and elevator pitches. "If we 'prep' each day by having a clear, concise story about our business – we'll be ready to go whether we are on a stage at a Live Event or simply sitting across the table from someone whom we want to take an interest in our business."

When I asked him about his experience in the Hot Seat and what he would do differently, Blair responded, "I might have been a little too passionate about my business and that energy should have been focused on my message. I don't know that my message was delivered as well as I had hoped." But he still benefited from the experience. "It gave me a kick in the pants!"

Blair reflected on his Hot Seat experience after the fact, analyzing the experience to see what he could take from it. "It was clear that I needed to 'pocket' my passion in those environments and be able to plainly state my business story and what problems I was looking to solve. Time with a smaller mastermind group allowed me to sit in a Hot Seat once again – except this time I had learned from my experience at the Live Event. I was able to map out my message and share a clear picture of my business with the group."

Although the moment on the Live Event Hot Seat was definitely *'hot'* for Blair, it proved to be beneficial as he continued to make progress with his business objectives.

"Hot Seats are not just limited to Live Events. They come in all forms – on stage in front of large groups of people, in small masterminds, during one-on-one conversation. The bottom line is that regardless of the format, you are speaking to people with whom you want to be prepared to tell your story and ask for what you need from the audience and explain how the other person will benefit. So be prepared to give them what they need to help you!"

Blair's Tips for Getting in the Hot Seat:

- Write down your biggest questions or problems and make copies for each person on the panel. Consider stapling something to the questions that will help the panelist identify YOU with the Questions (like a business card or something memorable from your business idea).

- Be Creative. Find out what resonates with the people on your panel and maybe provide a check with a donation to their charity as a gratitude gesture.

- But most importantly, just be you! Be genuine; don't try to be something you are not!

To Learn More About Blair Barnhardt and his vision to save America's Crumbling Roadways, please visit

www.drivingamericaforbetterroads.com

TO LEARN MORE ABOUT
EACH OF OUR SUCCESSFUL
HOT SEAT EXPERTS

VISIT
WWW.YOURBOOKBONUS.COM

SEE WHAT SPECIAL BONUS' ARE
WAITING FOR YOU!

WWW.YOURBOOKBONUS.COM
www.facebook.com/CarrieHartunianSmith

#BecauseOfMyBook

Around the Mike Koenig's and company community, writing a book comes up regularly in the marketing conversation. There are several ways that writing a book can benefits a person's business. It helps build credibility, can be used as a positioning tool, it's a great way to connect with people and of course, it's a great lead/revenue generator.

But there is yet another reason to write a book: because it is a passion project. Some of the most rewarding lessons I have learned came from listening to other people's stories. How they overcame life's challenges or how they were able to touch people's lives (or have their own lives changed).

Although *Hot Seat Conversations, Get Noticed, Get Tips, Get Going,* started as a pet project, it very quickly turned into a passion project. It became a way for me to connect with and hear from other people's real life experience. A way to connect and hear peoples real life, life changing stories first hand, so:

#Because Of My Book:

- I met and connected with some incredible people I would have more than likely never met - Thank You, Pam Bartha, Delina Fajardo, Blair Barnhardt and Joni Wilson!

- I strengthened relationships with amazing experts and entrepreneurs I call friends - Thank You Nobby Kleinman, Jim House, Joe Quartana, Debbie Owen and Andy Falco Jimenez!

- I was able to hear other people's purpose and passion and how it creates good will in the world we live in.

● I strengthened my personal convictions and goals as I continue down my journey.

● I found new life and purpose through other people's journeys.

Thank you to all the interviewees for enriching my life both personally and professionally.

About The Author

Carrie Hartunian Smith provides small businesses and entrepreneurs with what they are looking for: more LEADS, more REVENUE, and broader market REACH.

Carrie's professional experience allows her to confidently make such promises to her clients. Her passion for media and marketing has been the dominant thread of her professional life.

In 1993 Carrie joined a start-up media company that had one client bringing in $60K in monthly revenue. Within the first year the company had grown to over 20 accounts bringing in $8 million in annual revenue. That number had grown to nearly $100 million per year when the company was sold in 2007. Carrie stayed on with the new organization and was instrumental in advancing their aggressive acquisition strategy: 5 media companies acquired in 18 months, revenue increased to over $350 Million.

Achieving staggering results like these always comes with a cost, Carrie, a single mom, no longer willing to tolerate the insane corporate pace that those kind of results demanded.

So, in 2012, Carrie left her executive position and opened a consulting firm designed to work with people and organizations serious about making a huge impact to their bottom line and in their community. Carrie only works with organizations who are ready to make the necessary changes in their business, which will not only drive qualified clients to their business, but provide a higher quality of life outside of the business, enjoying what they like most in their leisure time.

The turning point in her transition from executive employee to entrepreneur came 18 months later when she "bumped" into Mike Koenigs, on his webinar, who she met and consulted with back in the early 2000's as she was growing the media company. With what she learned from becoming a Certified Consultant in both Top Gun and Traffic Geyser, Carrie was able to resuscitate a failing one time, $2K PPC campaign and transform it into a monthly consulting contract worth $7500 a month! As well as taking a 'buffet' style contract with another client, transforming it into a solid contract, doubling the initial amount, and adding monthly revenue opportunities.

Carrie is now living her dream of being a working 'stay-at-home' mom in Scottsdale, AZ!

She attributes becoming certified as TG 2.0/Top Gun and Marketing Roadmap Consultant as the cornerstones of her successful consulting business. As well as Mike Koenigs' Master Class, August 2014, with being able to write and publish this book in less than 14 days with 2 others in the pipeline.

To reach Carrie, you can find her on Facebook;

www.Facebook.com/ CarrieHartunianSmithConsultant